Poems for Year 5

Pie Corbett was a primary teacher and headteacher. He worked in teacher training and was English Inspector in Gloucestershire. He advises the National Literacy Strategy, especially on teaching poetry, writing and grammar. He writes training materials and has run Inservice across the country. The author of over a hundred books, a poet and storyteller, he spends much of his time irritating editors by not answering the phone because he is making up poems or daydreaming.

Poems for Year 3

chosen by
Pie Corbett

MACMILLAN CHILDREN'S BOOKS

First published 2002
by Macmillan Children's Books
a division of Macmillan Publishers Limited
20 New Wharf Road, London N1 9RR
Basingstoke and Oxford
www.panmacmillan.com

Associated companies throughout the world

ISBN 0 330 48288 2

A CIP catalogue record for this book is available from the British Library.
Printed by Mackays of Chatham plc, Chatham, Kent.

Contents

Introduction

An anthology is like a gathering of old friends. I'd like you to meet some of mine. Many of these poems I have known for a long time. They are so strong that the passing of time seems to have enriched their meaning. But there are also some new additions – fresh sparks that caught my eye like sudden gleams of sunlight. Sharply cut diamonds that reflect some facet of who we are.

I suppose I am lucky – my group of poetry friends is large. So, how was I to choose the sixty or so poems for this book? Well, in a way it was easy enough. At first hundreds of old chums jostled for attention. But I wanted poems that I had shared with children on many occasions. Poems that I knew would appeal, would interest and fascinate. Poems that would resonate in the mind long after their reading. So they had to be strong poems.

I wanted to bring together poems that were related – so that they would sometimes speak to each other in their own language, echoing back and forth across the pages. I wanted to have poems that I knew would not always be too easily grasped. Poems that might need thinking about. Not everything in life is easy to understand and sometimes the most mysterious are the most amazing – I could never fathom how a magnet works, but they have always fascinated me. Why don't rainbows wobble in the wind? Just because things are difficult to understand does not mean they cannot intrigue, or be

1

beautiful. Poems are not like simple sums – these old friends cannot always be tied down easily, but meet them, greet them and enjoy them.

And I wanted poems that could act as a kick-start to writing. Many of these poems are old standbys – faithful retainers, who have helped thousands of children find poetry within themselves, a self-confidence to put a word in, their word. Many of these poems have been the catalyst to children's own writing – and I have been lucky enough to witness some remarkable poems being written, in moments when something of our common genius poked its nose round the corner to surprise us all. So, I needed poems that I knew could strengthen imagination, release invention and ignite writing. If you like, this collection is a toolbox for creative teachers, readers and writers.

Finally, I imagined myself with a class of Year 3 children and thought about what poetry equipment we might need to take us through the journey of a year together. Poems that we could lean upon, poems that would surprise us, poems of many shades and moods. Poems that did not patronize. Poems that might light up a lifetime.

I wanted the poems to reflect the National Literacy Strategy. I thought it would be handy to have a good collection, easily accessible. So, there are poems based on close observation where the senses are attuned, shape poems that reflect their meaning, poems from different cultures, poems to chant aloud and perform, and humorous poetry that plays with language, including riddles, puns and word puzzles. All this is included – but, to be honest, while this helped to sharpen the choice, it never hindered. And besides, I wanted poems so strong that they would speak to others – those interested in writing in other year groups and beyond. Not just poems written for an eight year old, but poems that had demanded to be written.

So, step inside – meet this gathering of old friends and relations. Give them some time and you will get to know them well – and, maybe, make friends for life. You may even be tempted to create a few – take a step out of the darkness of yourself. Step into sunlight. It feels good to make new friends, to create something new.

Pie Corbett
April 2002

Prayer to Laughter

O Laughter
giver of relaxed mouths

you who rule our belly with tickles
you who come when not called
you who can embarrass us at times

send us stitches in our sides
shake us till the water reaches our eyes
buckle our knees till we cannot stand

we whose faces are grim and shattered
we whose hearts are no longer hearty
O Laughter we beg you

crack us up
crack us up

John Agard

The Merry Dance

When Wolf did a dance with Billy Goat white
Bear played the pipes with his paws,
The Ram began to brew some beer
While Cat washed up and licked her claws!

Trad. (Czech)

Translated by Valerie and
Andrew Fusek Peters

Wrong Rhyme

Little Bo-Peep has lost her sheep
And doesn't know where to find them
– *They've gone to the shops: there's a pile of lamb chops,*
With shoulders of mutton behind them.

Tony Charles

What Really Happened

Humpty Dumpty
Sat in the corner
While Little Jack Horner
Sat on a wall
But Little Miss Muffet
Stayed on her tuffet,
Not being frightened
Of spiders at all.

John Mole

Down Behind the Dustbin

Down behind the dustbin
I met a dog called Jim.
He didn't know me
And I didn't know him.

Michael Rosen

Big Fat Budgie

I'm a big fat budgie,
I don't do a lot.
Might park on my perch.
Might peck in my pot.
Might peek at my mirror.
Might ring my bell.
Might peer through the bars of my fat budgie cell.
Might say 'Who's a pretty boy then?'
Might not.
I'm a big fat budgie.
I don't do a lot.

Michaela Morgan

Chocolate Ants

If they started to sell
chocolate-covered ants
at the superstore
would you buy them?

If they gave them away
in a tasting test
would you try them?

If they said these are yummy,
and good for you too,
they keep away colds
and protect you from flu.

Would you say
you can give me
a packet or two.

And if you liked them
maybe you'd try . . .

and jelly slugs,
aniseed fleas
sugar-coated earwigs
or peppermint bugs

a range of tastes
waiting for you,
try 'Eleph-ants'
for a jumbo chew.

But I'd say no way –
I just couldn't,
could you?

Brian Moses

Alien Lullaby

Hush, little alien, don't you cry!
Mamma's gonna bake you a moonbeam pie

And if that moonbeam pie goes stale
Mamma's gonna catch you a comet's tail

And if that comet's tail won't flip
Mamma's gonna make you a rocket ship

And if that rocket ship won't stay
Mamma's gonna buy you the Milky Way

And if the Milky Way's too far
Mamma's gonna bring you a shooting star

And if that shooting star falls down –
You're still the sweetest little alien in town!

Sue Cowling

Nature's Numbers

One old observant owl
Two tame tickled trout
Three thirsty throated thrushes
Four fine fantailed fish
Five fantastically famous frogs
Six swiftly swimming salmon
Seven sweetly singing songbirds
Eight engagingly eager eels
Nine nippy and neighbourly
   newts
Ten tenderly tiptoeing tortoises.

John Cotton

In this Box

In this box I keep my secret
things like foreign coins with
holes in the   m, a rubber
in the sh   ape of an
elephant, a   thimble which
is made of   china and a
brass button that has an
eagle on it.   There are
other things I keep to myself.

Here is the key to
fit my box.

John Fairfax

Lion

I have a box
in which I keep
a shoulder I may cry on,
I lift the lid
and there inside's
a large and lovely lion.

My lion is wild
with glorious mane,
a pounce in every paw,
I have to keep
him in a box
for fear that he may roar.

The box is small,
you'd hardly think
the King of Beasts would fit,
I only keep
my lion there
by training him to sit.

From time to time
I lift the lid
to hear my lion purr,
and gently stroke
my fingers through
his soft and friendly fur.

I have a box
in which I keep
a secret to rely on,
so carefully close
the lid upon
my large and lovely lion.

Celia Warren

Wizard

Under my bed I keep a box
With seven locks,

And all the things I have to hide
Are safe inside:

My rings, my wand, my hat, my shells,
My book of spells.

I could fit a mountain into a shoe
If I wanted to,

Or put the sea in a paper cup
And drink it up.

I could change a cushion into a bird
With a magic word,

Or turn December into spring,
Or make stones sing,

I could clap my hands and watch the moon,
Like a white balloon,

Come floating to my window sill . . .
One day I will.

Richard Edwards

At the End of School Assembly

Miss Sparrow's lot flew out,
Mrs Steed's lot galloped out,
Mr Bull's lot got herded out,
Mrs Bumble's lot buzzed out.

Miss Rose's class . . . rose,
Mr Beetle's class . . . beetled off,
Miss Storm's class thundered out,
Mrs Frisby's class whirled across the hall.

Mr Train's lot made tracks,
Miss Ferry's lot sailed off,
Mr Roller's lot got their skates on,
Mrs Street's lot got stuck halfway across.

Mr Idle's class just couldn't be bothered,
Mrs Barrow's class were wheeled out,
Miss Stretcher's class were carried out
And
Mrs Brook's class
Simply
            trickled
                    away.

Simon Pitt

Rude Names for Nitwits

YOU   RAPSCALLION

FLIBBERTIGIBBET

FUSSBUDGET

COYSTRIL

TAYSTRIL

JOSKIN

BUMPKIN

CLOAF

CLODHOPPER

SLAMMERKIN

Alistair Reid

Ladles and Jellyspoons

Ladles and jellyspoons:
I come before you
To stand behind you
And tell you something
I know nothing about.

Next Thursday,
The day after Friday,
There'll be a ladies' meeting
For men only.

Wear your best clothes
If you haven't any,
And if you can come
Please stay home.

Admission is free,
You can pay at the door.
We'll give you a seat
So you can sit on the floor.

It makes no difference
Where you sit;
The kid in the gallery
Is sure to spit.

Anon.

Who's That on the Phone?
('Lobster Telephone' by Salvador Dali)

There's a lobster on the phone!

Not a crayfish
Or a seal,
Not a spider crab
Or an eel –
But a lobster!

Not a mobster
Full of threats,
Nor debt collector
seeking debts –
But a lobster!

Not a salesgirl,
Double-glazing
Nor astrologer,
future-gazing –
But a lobster!

Not an emu
On the loose,
Nor a zebra,
Nor a moose,
Not a hangman
With a noose . . .

No, there's a lobster on the phone
And he wants to speak to you!

Pie Corbett

I Ask You!

Does a catalogue ever have kittens?
Or do foxgloves ever grow mittens?
Does a cowslip ever moo?

Can a dog rose jump up and bark?
Or a cricket bat fly after dark?
Ever seen a football in a shoe?

I ask you!

When do pussy willows ever start purring?
Or a buttercup ever need stirring?
Does a dandelion live in a zoo?

Will a moonstone ever start shining?
Or a dinosaur ever stop dining?
Ever heard a catkin saying 'Mew'?

I ask you!

Does a kitchen sink ever float?
Can you toot the horns of a goat?
Does a hare ever have a shampoo?

Does a crowbar need a big nest?
Must a sunflower set in the west?
Do sweet peas go in a stew?

I ask you!

Must a bluebottle have a cork?
Can a rambling rose get up and walk?
Does a lyre ever play true?

Have you heard a monkey nut chattering?
Or a reindeer pitter-pattering?
Can a weathercock say 'Doodle Doo'?

I've never heard of such things.

I ask you – Have you?

David Whitehead

The Schoolkids' Rap

Miss was at the blackboard writing with the chalk,
When suddenly she stopped in the middle of her talk.
She snapped her fingers – snap! snap! snap!
Pay attention children and I'll teach you how to rap.

She picked up a pencil, she started to tap.
All together children, now clap! clap! clap!
Just get the rhythm, just get the beat.
Drum it with your fingers, stamp it with your feet.

That's right children, keep in time.
Now we've got the rhythm, all we need is the rhyme.
This school is cool. Miss Grace is ace.
Strut your stuff with a smile on your face.

Snap those fingers, tap those toes.
Do it like they do it on the video shows.
Flap it! Slap it! Clap! Snap! Clap!
Let's all do the schoolkids' rap!

John Foster

My Dad's Amazing!

My Dad's AMAZING for he can:

make mountains out of molehills,
teach Granny to suck eggs,
make Mum's blood boil,
and then drive her up the wall.

My Dad's AMAZING for he also:

walks around with his head in the clouds,
has my sister eating out of his hand,
says he's got eyes in the back of his head
and can read me like a book.

BUT,
the most AMAZING thing of all is:

when he's caught someone red-handed
first he jumps down their throat
and then he bites their head off!

Ian Souter

Mum's Infallible Method for Solving Arguments about Who Gets the Biggest Slice of Cream Cake

I'll make sure
no one loses;
you cut,
she chooses!

Judith Nicholls

My Dream

I dreamed a dream next Tuesday week,
Beneath the apple trees;
I thought my eyes were big pork pies
And my nose was Stilton cheese.
The clock struck twenty minutes to six,
When a frog sat on my knee;
I asked him to lend me eighteen pence,
But he borrowed a shilling off me.

Anon.

Tall Dreams

A baby giraffe's dreams are tall,

of licking ice-cream clouds

and tiptoeing over treetops.

Brian Morse

Snow Dreams

Snow slides over hill and forest,
ices rooftops,
muffles the land.

Behind the white-cloaked fir,
remembering his childhood,
an old man hides
in silence,
snowball in hand.

Judith Nicholls

The Famous Five

Please speak to me, ears.
Give me the sound of water over stones.
And you too, eyes,
Don't hang around staring at the floor!
Show me again how in those far off fields
The light falls like sheets of gold.
And nose, poor nose, subject of so many jokes,
Bring the scents of my childhood to haunt me:
The smell of privet hedges,
The tang
Of an estuary.
The scent of my mother's dress.
And you, touch,
Let me feel my friend's breath on my skin,
Falling there like a web of peace.
Tongue, remind me of what the earth tastes like.
And, while you're about it,
Tell me the words of the spell
That will stop the world from shrinking.
Ears, can you hear the spell?
Eyes, can you see if it's working?
Nose, please sniff out the truth.

Brian Patten

Listen

Silence is when you can hear things.
Listen:
The breathing of bees,
A moth's footfall,
Or the mist easing its way
Across the field,
The light shifting at dawn
Or the stars clicking into place
At evening.

John Cotton

In the Kitchen

In the kitchen
After the aimless
Chatter of the plates,
The murmuring of the gas,
The chuckles of the water pipes
And the sharp exchanges
Of the knives, forks and spoons,
Comes the serious quiet
When the sink slowly clears its throat,
And you can hear the occasional rumble
Of the refrigerator's tummy
As it digests the cold.

John Cotton

Here Comes the Ssh Patrol

The Ssh Patrol
tiptoe to a
silent theme tune,
played on stringless guitar
and skinless drum.

On their backs
are hush packs
of special equipment.
Tongue tiers
Shout clippers
Scream mufflers

They capture the crackles in newspapers
Steal the creaks on staircases
and oil gravel.

When their tasks are complete
They give their Secret Salute –
Fingers on lips
and slip silently away.

John Coldwell

The Lost Voice

Your grandpa's lost his voice,
They said. You mustn't
Make him try to talk.

And so we sat through tea
While words flew all around him
About this and that . . .

His eyes kept going back and forth
And side to side as if
he didn't want to miss a syllable

But I knew better. This
Was serious, an old man
Searching for his voice

Who could not find it.

John Mole

The Sound Collector

A stranger called this morning
Dressed all in black and grey
Put every sound into a bag
And carried them away

The whistling of the kettle
The turning of the lock
The purring of the kitten
The ticking of the clock

The popping of the toaster
The crunching of the flakes
When you spread the marmalade
The scraping noise it makes

The hissing of the frying-pan
The ticking of the grill
The bubbling of the bathtub
As it starts to fill

The drumming of the raindrops
On the window pane
When you do the washing up
The gurgle of the drain

The crying of the baby
The squeaking of the chair
The swishing of the curtain
The creaking of the stair

A stranger called this morning
He didn't leave his name
Left us only silence
Life will never be the same.

Roger McGough

Full

The day's
as full of possibilities
as of light.

Sun high already
cutting the mist apart
under shadowed
trees.

Rupert M. Loydell

What is the Sun?

the Sun is an orange dinghy
   sailing across a calm sea
it is a gold coin
   dropped down a drain in
     Heaven
the Sun is a yellow beach ball
   kicked high into the summer
     sky
it is a red thumbprint
   on a sheet of pale blue paper
the Sun is a milk bottle's gold top
   floating in a puddle.

Wes Magee

When Day Breaks

When
 d
            y
      a
            breaks

Who gets up to fix it?

James Carter

Autumn Thought

Flowers are happy in summer.
In autumn they die and are blown away.
　　Dry and withered,
Their petals dance on the wind
Like little brown butterflies.

Langston Hughes

Autumn Riddle Haiku

Paw prints in the lane.
Starfish far from home.
Pattern the ground.

Pie Corbett

From a Dakota Wheat-Field

Like liquid gold the wheat-field lies,
  A marvel of yellow and russet and green,
That ripples and runs, that floats and flies,
  With the subtle shadows, the change,
    the sheen,
  That play in the golden hair of a girl –
    A ripple of amber – a flare
  Of light sweeping after – a curl
  In the hollows like swirling feet
    Of fairy waltzers, the colours run
    To the western sun
  Through the deeps of
      the ripening wheat.

Hamlin Garland

To Make a Prairie

To make a prairie it takes a clover
and one bee,
One clover, and a bee.
And revery.
The revery alone will do,
If bees are few.

Emily Dickinson

Making the Countryside

Take a roll of green,
Spread it under a blue or blue-grey sky,
Hollow out a valley, mould hills.

Let a river run through the valley,
Let fish swim in it, let dippers
Slide along is surface.

Spring cows in the water meadows,
Cover steep banks with trees,
Let foxes sleep beneath and owls
   above.

Now, let the seasons turn,
Let everything follow its course.
Let it be.

June Crebbin

Inside the Morning

Inside the morning is a bird,
Inside the bird is a song,
Inside the song is a longing,

And the longing is to fill the morning.

June Crebbin

The Inside of Things

Inside the dandelion seed is a clock,
Inside the egg is a chicken farm;
Inside a fist an army awaits,
Inside a kiss is an open palm.

Inside a snowflake an avalanche
Trembles and waits to get free;
Inside a raindrop a river plots
The best way to run to the sea.

Brian Patten

Wind

I pulled a hummingbird out of the sky one day but let it go,
I heard a song and carried it with me on my cotton streamers,
I dropped it on an ocean and lifted up a wave with my bare
  hands,
I made a whole canefield tremble and bend as I ran by,
I pushed a soft cloud from here to there,
I hurried a stream along a pebbled path,
I scooped up a yard of dirt and hurled it in the air,
I lifted a straw hat and sent it flying,
I broke a limb from a guava tree,
I became a breeze, bored and tired,
and hovered and hung and rustled and lay where I could.

Dionne Brand

Windy Nights

Rumbling in the chimneys,
Rattling at the doors,
Round the roofs and round the roads
The rude wind roars;
Raging through the darkness,
Raving through the trees,
Racing off again across
The great grey seas.

Rodney Bennett

Robin Song

I am the hunted king
  Of the frost and big icicles
    And the bogey cold
    With its wind boots.

I am the uncrowned
  Of the rainworld
    Hunted by lightning and thunder
    And rivers.

I am the lost child
  Of the wind
    Who goes through me looking for something
      else
    Who can't recognize me though I cry.

I am the maker
  Of the world
    That rolls to crush
    And silence my knowledge.

                              Ted Hughes

Snow

There's the old woman plucking her geese
And selling the feathers a penny apiece.

They're killing geese in Scotland
And sending the feathers down here.

Trad. (Yorkshire)

Kit's First Snow

His world had gone
Overnight –
Paths, tracks, known smells
All sunk
Under soft whiteness
That made him wince and sneeze.
Packed footmarks showed
Where the milkman had trod;
A second set, the postman's.
Kit, on flinching paws,
Quickstepped to the gate
In a dazzle of white.
Couldn't see where it ended
So stood up to stare,
Poised like a meerkat.

An exclamation in the snow –
Black kitten
In a white world.

Linda Newbery

Chips

Out of the paper bag
Comes the hot breath of the
  chips
And I shall blow on them
To stop them burning my lips.

Before I leave the counter
The woman shakes
Raindrops of vinegar on them
And salty snowflakes.

Outside the frosty pavements
Are slippery as a slide
But the chips and I
Are warm inside.

Stanley Cook

No one Made Mash Like My Grandad!

With a fork and some
pepper, butter and cream –

in front of the fire
he whipped up a dream.

Rupert M. Loydell

I Asked the Little Boy
Who Cannot See

I asked the little boy who cannot see,
'And what is colour like?'
'Why, green,' said he,
'Is like the rustle when the wind blows through
The forest; running water, that is blue;
And red is like a trumpet sound; and pink
Is like the smell of roses; and I think
That purple must be like a thunderstorm;
And yellow is like something soft and warm;
And white is pleasant stillness when you lie
And dream.'

Anon.

Paint

I should like to paint
the eye of a raindrop
the foot of a thunderclap
the heart of a cloud

the roving eye of dew
clawed foot of lightning
the elastic heart of cumulus

paint
a mascara-ed eye
a sultry heart
a silken foot

then
black cloud
forked lightning
a splintered raindrop

a squall of rain
wet hair on a brow
a dubious eye

A finger of rain walking across a sodden field to
a fringe of wood where a majestic tree is falling

Brian Morse

I Saw a Peacock

I saw a peacock with a fiery tail.
I saw a blazing comet drop down hail.
I saw a cloud with ivy circled round.
I saw a sturdy oak creep on the ground.
I saw a little ant swallow a whale.
I saw a raging sea brim full of ale.
I saw a drinking glass sixteen feet deep.
I saw a well full of men's tears that weep.
I saw their eyes all in a flame of fire.
I saw a house as big as Moon and higher.
I saw the sun in the middle of night.
I saw the man that saw this wondrous sight.

Anon.

I Am a Glorious Star

I am a glowing star, *make me the silver planet.*
I am a dirty rag, *make me the red carpet.*
I am a piece of mattress, *make me the four-poster bed.*
I am a tiny match, *make me the raging fire.*
I am a hot light bulb, *make me the flaming sun.*
I am a flake of snow, *make me the snow queen.*
I am a clear raindrop, *make me the colour-filled rainbow.*
I am a shivering small girl, *make me the powerful giant.*

Tania Colley

Nocturnophobia

I am scared of the dark.

Like car tyres are afraid of the lost nail,
Like the salmon is afraid of the poacher's net,
Like a cat is afraid of the car's hot roar
Like the forest is afraid of the slightest spark,
Like the fields of barley are afraid of the
    locust swarm,
Like the actor is afraid of the forgotten word,
Like the model's face is afraid of the jagged
    glass,
Like the relationship is afraid of the jealous
    thought,
Like the heart is afraid of the final STOP.

What are you afraid of?

Pie Corbett and
Gloucestershire children

This is the Day

This is the sort of day
I should like to wrap
In shiny silver paper
And only open when it's raining,

This is the sort of day
I should like to hide
In a secret drawer to which
Only I have the key,

This is the sort of day
I should like to hang
At the back of the wardrobe
To keep me warm when winter comes,

This is the day
I should like to last forever,

This is my birthday.

June Crebbin

Rhyme-Time

Our teacher, Mrs Paradigm,
To teach us children how to rhyme,
Has asked us all to take our name
And find a word that sounds the
    same.
And so we did.

Andy is dandy,
Bhupa is super
Kitty is pretty and
Clare is fair.
Mabel is able
Scott is hot,
Luke is cute but
Danuta is cuter.
Dwight is bright,
Trevor is clever
Terry is merry and
Jim is slim.
Brenda is tender
Cecil is special,
Dean is keen but
Rowena is keener.
Liz is a whizz
Danny is canny
Pip is hip and
Gill is brill,

Holly is jolly
Grace is ace
Pete is sweet but
Nita is sweeter.
Kate is great,
Mick is quick,
Nancy is fancy and
Paul is tall.
Sally is pally,
Wendy is trendy
Dave is brave but
Fraser is braver.

The trouble is my name is Matt,
And I can't think of a rhyme for that.
Well, not a nice one anyway!

Gervase Phinn

The Name of the Game

Play with names
And Pat becomes tap.
Karl is a lark
And Pam is a map.

Miles is smile.
Liam is mail.
Bart is a brat.
Lina's a nail.

Stan tans.
Gary turns gray.
Norma's a Roman.
Amy makes May.

Tabitha's habitat.
Leon is lone.
Kate is teak.
Mona's a moan.

Trish is a shirt.
Kay is a yak.
But whatever you do,
Jack remains Jack.

John Foster

Give Me a House

Give me a house, said Polly.
Give me land, said Hugh.
Give me the moon, said Sadie.
Give me the sun, said Sue.

Give me a horse, said Rollo.
Give me a hound, said Joe.
Give me fine linen, said Sarah.
Give me silk, said Flo.

Give me a mountain, said Kirsty.
Give me a valley, said Jim.
Give me a river, said Dodo.
Give me the sky, said Tim.

Give me the ocean, said Adam.
Give me a ship, said Hal.
Give me a kingdom, said Rory.
Give me a crown, said Sal.

Give me gold, said Peter.
Give me silver, said Paul.
Give me love, said Jenny,
Or nothing at all.

Charles Causley

My Name Is . . .

My name is Sluggery-wuggery
My name is Worms-for-tea
My name is Swallow-the-table-leg
My name is Drink-the-sea.

My name is I-eat-saucepans
My name is I-like-snails
My name is Grand-piano-George
My name is I-ride-whales.

My name is Jump-the-chimney
My name is Bite-my-knee
My name is Jiggery-pokery
And Riddle-me-ree, and ME.

Pauline Clarke

You!

You!
Your head is like a hollow drum.
You!
Your eyes are like balls of flame.
You!
Your ears are like fans for blowing fire.
You!
Your nostril is like a mouse's hole.
You!
Your mouth is like a lump of mud.
You!
Your hands are like drumsticks.
You!
Your belly is like a pot of bad water.
You!
Your legs are like wooden posts.
You!
Your backside is like a mountain top.

Igbo

The Jolly Gentleman

I say I say
I say what what
what what
I say I say

I am a jolly
gentleman
and I bid you
all
good day

John Mole

I Saw a Jolly Hunter

I saw a jolly hunter
With a jolly gun
Walking in the country
in the jolly sun.

In the jolly meadow
Sat a jolly hare.
Saw the jolly hunter.
Took jolly care.

Hunter jolly eager –
Sight of jolly prey.
Forgot gun pointing
Wrong jolly way.

Jolly hunter jolly head
Over heels gone.
Jolly old safety catch
Not jolly on.

Bang went the jolly gun.
Hunter jolly dead.
Jolly hare got clean
    away.
Jolly good, I said.

Charles Causley

Python on Piccolo

Python on piccolo,
Dingo on drums,
Gannet on gee-tar*
Sits and strums.

Croc on cornet
Goes to town,
Sloth on sitar
Upside-down.

Toad on tuba
Sweet and strong,
Crane on clarinet,
Goat on gong.
          And the sun jumped up in the morning.

Toucan travelling
On trombone,
Zebra zapping.
On xylophone.

Beaver on bugle
Late and soon,
Boa constrictor
On bassoon.

Tiger on trumpet
Blows a storm,
Flying fox
On flügelhorn.
>   *And the sun jumped up in the morning.*

Frog on fiddle,
Hippo on harp,
Owl on oboe
Flat and sharp.

Viper on vibes
Soft and low,
Pelican
on pi-a-no.

Dromedary
On double-bass,
Cheetah on cello
Giving chase.
>   *And the sun jumped up in the morning.*

>   *Charles Causley*

* *guitar*

Tiger Shadows

I wish I was a tiger in the Indian jungle
The jungle would be my teacher

No school
And the night sky a blackboard smudged with stars
I wish I was a tiger in the Indian jungle

Kitten-curious
I'd pad about on paws big as frying pans

While the monkeys chatted in the trees above me
I'd sniff the damp jungly air
Out of exotic flowers I would make a crown of pollen

If I were a tiger in the Indian jungle
My eyes would glitter among the dark green leaves
My tail would twitch like a snake

I would discover abandoned cities
Where no human feet had trod for centuries

I would be lord of a lost civilization
And leap among the vine-covered ruins

I wish I was a tiger in the Indian jungle
As the evening fell
I'd hum quiet tiger-tunes to which the fireflies would dance
I'd watch the red, bubbling sun
Go fishing with its net of shadows

While the hunters looked for me miles and miles away
I'd like stretched out in my secret den

I would doze in the strawberry-coloured light
Under the golden stripy shadows of the trees
I would dream a tiger's dream

Brian Patten

The Tomcat

At midnight in the alley
A Tomcat comes to wail,
And he chants the hate of a million years
As he swings his snaky tail.

Malevolent, bony, brindled,
Tiger and devil and bard,
His eyes are coals from the middle of Hell
And his heart is black and hard.

He twists and crouches and capers
And bares his curved sharp claws,
And he sings to the stars of the jungle nights,
Ere cities were, or laws.

Beast from a world primeval,
He and his leaping clan,
When the blotched red moon leers over the roofs,
Give voice to their scorn of man.

He will lie on a rug tomorrow
And lick his silky fur,
And veil the brute in his yellow eyes
And play he's tame, and purr.

But at midnight in the alley
He will crouch again and wail,
And beat the time for his demon's song,
With the swing of his demon's tail.

Don Marquis

The Loch Ness Monster's Song

Sssnnnwhuffffll?
Hnwhuffl hhnnwfl hnfl hfl?
Gdroblboblhobngbl gbl gl g g g g glbgl.
Drublhaflablhaflubhafgabhaflhafl fl fl –
gm grawwwww grf grawf awfgm graw gm.
Hovoplodok-doplodovok-plovodokot-doplodokosh?
Splgraw fok fok splgrafhatchgabrlgabrl fok splfok!
Zgra kra gka fok!
Grof grawff gahf?
Gombl mlb bl –
blm plm,
blm plm,
blm plm,
blp.

Edwin Morgan

Cautionary Playground Rhyme

Natasha Green
Natasha Green
stuck her head in a washing machine

Washing Machine
Washing Machine
round and round Natasha Green

Natasha Green
Natasha Green
cleanest girl I've ever seen

Ever Seen
Ever seen
A girl with her head in a washing machine?

Washing Machine
Washing Machine
last home of Natasha Green

Natasha Green
Natasha Green
washed away in a white machine

White Machine
White Machine
soaped to death Natasha Green

Natasha Green
Natasha Green
cleanest ghost I've ever seen!

MORAL:

Washing machines are for knickers and blouses
Washing machines are for jumpers and trousers
Keep your head out of the washing machine
or you'll end up as spotless as little Miss Green.

Ian McMillan

Miss Mary

Miss Mary	she asked her	He jumped so
Mack	mother	high
Mack	mother	high
Mack	mother	high
all dressed in	for fifty	he reached the
black	cents	sky
black	cents	sky
black	cents	sky
with silver	to watch the	he didn't come
buttons	elephant	down
buttons	elephant	down
buttons	elephant	down
all down her	jump the	till the fifth of Ju—
back	fence	ly
back	fence	ly
back	fence.	ly.

Anon. (USA)

81

Overheard on a Saltmarsh

Nymph, nymph, what are your beads?
Green glass, goblin. Why do you stare at them?
Give them me.

No.

Give them me. Give them me.

No.

Then I will howl all night in the reeds.
Lie in the mud and howl for them.

Goblin, why do you love them so?

They are better than stars or water,
Better than voices of winds that sing,
Better than any man's fair daughter,
Your green glass beads on a silver ring.

Hush, I stole them out of the moon.

Give me your beads, I desire them.

No.

I will howl in a deep lagoon
For your green glass beads, I love them so.
Give them me. Give them.

No.

Harold Monro

Fairy Glen

Down deep in the glen
  where the fairies play,
the tall trees stretch
  by star, by day.
But deep in the glen
  where the fairies hide
the waters are cold
  and the waters are wide.

Down deep in the glen
  where the fairies fly,
the swift swallow swoops
  in a cloudless sky.
But deep in the glen
  where the fairies prance
the waterfall laughs
  in its otherworld dance.

Down deep in the glen
  where the fairies run,
the grey rocks bask
  in a summer-high sun.
But deep in the glen
  where the fairies peek,
the bat wings flap
  and the sly snakes
    sneak.

Down deep in the glen
   where the fairies frown,
the river runs rogue
   – a child might drown.
Down deep in the glen
   where the fairies leap,
a fairy wing wraps
   a child to keep.

John Rice

Phinniphin

The tide is in,
  The tide is in,
    The Phinniphin
    Are out.

They love the sea,
  The salty sea,
    Of this there is
    No doubt.

O watch them flop
  And slip and slop
    With clumsy hop
    Right past

The sandy beach
  Until they reach
    The friendly sea
    At last.

But when the tide,
  The shifty tide
    Stays right outside
    The bar,

They can't go in
The Phinniphin;
The Phinniphin
Cannot go in:
They'd have to hop
Too far.

Frank Collymore

The Beach

The beach is a quarter of golden fruit,
a soft ripe melon
sliced to a half-moon curve,
having a thick green rind
of jungle growth;
and the sea devours it
with its sharp white teeth.

W. Hart-Smith

Beach

Dry whisper of seagrass.
My feet and legs are bare.
Strong and steady stiff sea wind
is tearing at my hair.
Cold sun's hand across the land
bleached and pale as bone.
Sandscape, landscape lunar dunes
blown for me alone.

Ann Bonner

My Song

Sitting, legs crossed, copper-toned old man
Chanting in low bass.
  'Ho aa Hey yah'
  'Way ah Hey ah'
Black Wolf is singing to the morning.
  'Hey aa ah Hey'
  'Way ah Hey aa'
He is singing to many years ago.
  'Hey ah Way Hey'
  'Way ah Hey aa'
The singing stops
Drum silent.
Black Wolf looks down at his drum.
He has sung.

King D. Kuka
American Indian (Blackfoot)

Sampan

Waves lap lap
Fish fins clap clap
Brown sails flap flap
Chopsticks tap tap
Up and down the long green river
Ohe Ohe lanterns quiver
Willow branches brush the river
Ohe Ohe lanterns quiver
Waves lap lap
Fish fins clap clap
Brown sails flap flap
Chopsticks tap tap

Tao Lang Pee (Chinese)

'Bye Now

Walk good
Walk good
Noh mek macca go juk yu
Or cow go buk yu,
Noah mek dog bite yu
Or hungry go ketch yu, yah!

Noh mek sunhot turn yu dry.
No mek rain soak yu.
Noh mek tief tief yu.
Or stone go buck yu foot, yah!
Walk good
Walk good

James Berry

Goodbye Now

Walk well
Walk well
Don't let thorns run in you
Or let a cow butt you.
Don't let a dog bite you
Or hunger catch you, hear!

Don't let sun's heat turn you dry.
Don't let rain soak you.
Don't let thief rob you
Or a stone bump your foot, hear!
Walk well
Walk well

James Berry

Bells of Rhymney

O what can you give me?
Say the sad bells of Rhymney.

Is there hope for the future?
Cry the brown bells of Merthyr.

Who made the mineowner?
Say the black bells of Rhondda.

And who robbed the miner?
Cry the grim bells of Blaina.

They will plunder willy-nilly,
Say the bells of Caerphilly.

They have fangs, they have teeth!
Shout the loud bells of Neath.

To the south, things are sullen,
Say the pink bells of Brecon.

Even God is uneasy,
Say the moist bells of Swansea.

Put the vandals in court!
Cry the bells of Newport.

All would be well if— if— if—
Say the green bells of Cardiff.

Why so worried, sisters, why?
Sing the silver bells of Wye.

Idris Davies

Blessings

Bless the blue sky,
bright as a bride.
Bless the clear sea,
and creatures that hide.

Bless the deep sleep,
sweet with a dream.
Bless every flower
and the fresh stream.

Bless the sun's glow
and the plant's green.
Bless the proud earth,
the eagle's scream.

Bless the Scots thistle
and the slithery snake.
Bless the smooth fish
that swims in the lake.

Bless every spring,
leaf, stalk and frond.
Bless the spotted egg,
splashes in a pond.

Bless the stray dog,
the tramp in the road.
Bless twice the poor
and their heavy load.

Dennis Carter

A Heart

A heart to hate you
Is as far as the moon.
A heart to love you
Is near as the door.

Trad. (Burundi)

If I Lived

If I lived in a terrace house, traffic
would shake me.

If I lived in a castle keep, the wind
would wake me.

If I lived in a bungalow, I'd sleep
downstairs.

If I lived in a tower block, I'd fly
high in the air.

If I lived in a boat, I'd float
on slow green water.

If I lived in a caravan, I'd be
the traveller's daughter.

Gillian Clarke

Inside My Head

Inside my head there's a forest,
A castle, a cottage, a king,
A rose, a thorn, some golden hair,
A turret, a tower, a ring.

A horse, a prince, a secret word,
A giant, a gaol, a pond,
A witch, a snake, a bubbling pot,
A wizard, a warlock, a wand.

Inside my head there's an ocean,
A parrot, a pirate, a gull,
A cave, a sword, a silver coin,
A princess, an island, a skull.

A ghost, a ghoul, a creaking stair,
A shadow, a shudder, a shout,
A flame, a grave, a swirling mist,
A rainbow, an angel, a cloud.

Inside my head there's a country
Of mountains and valleys and streams,
It all comes alive when I listen
To stories, to poems, to dreams.

Steve Turner

Acknowledgements

The compiler and publishers wish to thank the following for permission to use copyright material:

John Agard, 'Prayer to Laughter' from *Laughter is an Egg* by John Agard, Viking (1990), by permission of Caroline Sheldon Literary Agency on behalf of the author; **James Berry**, 'Goodbye Now' and 'Bye Now' from *When I Dance* by James Berry, Hamish Hamilton (1988), by permission of PFD on behalf of the author; **Ann Bonner**, 'Beach', by permission of the author; **Dennis Carter**, 'Blessings' from *Sleeplessness Jungle* by Dennis Carter, Clwyd Poetry Project (1998), by permission of the author; **James Carter**, 'When Day Breaks', by permission of the author; **Charles Causley**, 'Python on Piccolo', 'I Saw a Jolly Hunter' and 'Give Me a House' from *Collected Poems* by Charles Causley, Macmillan, by permission of David Higham Associates on behalf of the author; **Tony Charles**, 'Wrong Rhymes', by permission of the author; **Gillian Clarke**, 'If I Lived' from *The Animal Wall* by Gillian Clarke, Pont Books, Gomer Press (1990), by permission of the author; **Pauline Clarke**, 'My Name Is . . .' from *Silver Bells and Cockle Shells* by Pauline Clarke. Copyright © Pauline Clarke, 1962, by permission of Curtis Brown on behalf of Peter Hunter Blair; **John Coldwell**, 'Here Comes the Sssh Patrol', by permission of the author; **John Cotton**, 'Listen', 'Nature's Numbers' and 'In the Kitchen', by permission of the author; **Sue Cowling**, 'Alien Lullaby' from *Space Poems*, Oxford University Press (2002), by permission of the author; **June Crebbin**, 'This is the Day' from *The Dinosaur's Dinner* by June Crebbin, Viking (1992), by per-

Children's Books (1996), by permission of the author; **Harold Monro**, 'Overheard on a Saltmarsh' from *Collected Harold Monro*, by permission of Gerald Duckworth & Co Ltd; **Edwin Morgan**, 'The Loch Ness Monster's Song' from *Collected Poems* by Edwin Morgan, by permission of Carcanet Press Ltd; **Michaela Morgan**, 'Big Fat Budgie', first published in *The Hairy Hamster Hunt*, compiled by Tony Bradman, Macdonald Young Books, by permission of the author; **Brian Morse**, 'Paint' from *Picnic on the Moon* by Brian Morse, Macmillan (1993), and 'Tall Dreams', by permission of the author; **Brian Moses**, 'Chocolate Ants' from *I Wish I Could Dine With a Porcupine* by Brian Moses, Hodder/Wayland (2000), by permission of the author; **Linda Newbery**, 'Kit's First Snow', by permission of Maggie Noach Literary Agency on behalf of the author; **Judith Nicholls**, 'Mum's Infallible Method For Solving Arguments About Who Gets The Biggest Slice of Cream Cake' and 'Snow Dreams'. Copyright © Judith Nicholls 2002, by permission of the author; **Brian Patten**, 'The Famous Five', 'The Inside of Things' and 'Tiger Shadows' from *Juggling With Jerbils* by Brian Patten, Puffin Books (2000). Copyright © Brian Patten 2000, by permission of Rogers, Coleridge & White on behalf of the author; **Andrew Fusek Peters**, 'The Merry Dance', trad. Czech, translated by Andrew Fusek Peters and Vera Fusek Peters, from *Sheep Don't Go to School*, ed. Andrew Fusek Peters, Bloodaxe (1999), by permission of the author; **Gervase Phinn**, 'Rhyme-Time', by permission of the author; **Simon Pitt**, 'At the End of School Assembly', first published in *The Bees Squeeze*, ed. Gary Boswell, Stride (1990), by permission of the author; **Alastair Reid**, 'Rude Words for Nitwits' from *Ounce Dice Trice*' by Alistair Reid, Atlantic/Little Brown (1958), by permission of the author; **John Rice**, 'Fairy Glen' from *The*

Dream of Night Fishers, Scottish Cultural Press (1998), by permission of the author; **Michael Rosen**, 'Down Behind the Dustbin' from *Wouldn't You Like to Know* by Michael Rosen, Andre Deutsch (1977), by permission of PFD on behalf of the author; **Ian Souter**, 'My Dad's Amazing', by permission of the author; **Steve Turner**, 'Inside My Head' from *The Day I Fell Down the Toilet* by Steve Turner, Lion Publishing (1996), by permission of the author; **Celia Warren**, 'Lion', first published in *Hippo Book of Magic Poems*, ed. J Curry, Scholastic (1997), by permission of the author; **David Whitehead**, 'I Ask You', by permission of the author.